A QUIET SPACE

A Quiet Space

A Short History of the Sanctuary

SR STAN KENNEDY
AND SR SÍLE WALL

VERITAS

Published 2023 by
Veritas Publications
7–8 Lower Abbey Street
Dublin 1
Ireland
publications@veritas.ie
www.veritas.ie

ISBN 978 1 80097 076 2

www.sanctuary.ie

10 9 8 7 6 5 4 3 2

Designed and typeset by Padraig McCormack, Veritas
Publications
Printed in the Republic of Ireland by Walsh Colour Print, Kerry

Veritas Publications is a member of Publishing Ireland.

*Veritas books are printed on paper made from the wood pulp of
managed forests. For every tree felled, at least one tree is planted,
thereby renewing natural resources.*

This book is dedicated to the many thousands of people who have contributed in various ways to the life of the Sanctuary over the years.

A wooden stool in the
Contemplative Garden

A quiet space.
A silent space.
A still space.

**Síle Wall, 'The Sanctuary's
Flowering Quince Remembers'**

Contents

Acknowledgements   11

Preface
by Sr Stan Kennedy
and Sr Síle Wall   13

Reflection
by Gary Graham   15

Reflection
by Jane Negrych   17

Introduction
by Tony Bates   21

Part 1
The Story of the Sanctuary   27

Part 2
The Pillars of the Sanctuary   51
» Spirituality   53
» Meditation   61
» Creativity   69
» Community   75

Poem by Síle Wall
The Sanctuary's Flowering
    Quince Remembers   87

Conclusion   91

Sanctuary staff, 2023. From left to right: Johanne Farrelly, Patricia Rodriguez, John Robinson, Nikki Solyom, Jane Negrych, Pat Sheridan and Anita Dobulane (missing: Mary O'Grady, Paul Byrne, Louise Ward and Bernadette Mac Ceallaigh)

Acknowledgements

We are immensely grateful to everyone who has worked with us over the last quarter-century: staff, board members and volunteers. Our deepest thanks to our current board of directors: Tony Bates, Pat Dennigan, Gary Graham, Liam MacGabhann and Jean O'Kelly, and our current team of staff: Paul Byrne, Anita Dobulane, Johanne Farrelly, Bernadette Mac Ceallaigh,

Jane Negrych, Mary O'Grady, John Robinson, Patricia Rodriguez, Pat Sheridan, Nikki Solyom and Louise Ward.

A special thanks to Siobhán Parkinson for editing the first draft, to Johanne Farrelly for her help with the book, to Maria Gallagher of re:design for her artwork, to Síne Quinn, Veritas Publications, for her support and encouragement, and to Fiona Dunne, Padraig McCormack and all the team at Veritas Publications who carefully edited and designed the book.

All royalties from the sale of this book will go towards furthering the work of the Sanctuary.

Mary Aikenhead, founder of the Religious Sisters of Charity. Image credit: The Religious Sisters of Charity

Preface

The story of the Sanctuary evolves from the story of Mary Aikenhead (1787–1858), who lived in Stanhope Street over two hundred years ago. She founded the Religious Sisters of Charity, the congregation to which the founders of the Sanctuary belong.

Mary Aikenhead was a woman of deep spirituality and great compassion who responded to the needs of her time with foresight and courage. She was prophetic in responding to needs other people didn't yet recognise. When establishing the first Catholic hospital run by nuns in Ireland, she was very clear that it was to be open to people of all faiths – and none.

Mary Aikenhead is a model and an inspiration for the work of the Sanctuary. Like her, we at the Sanctuary respond to hidden need – the social, psychological and spiritual needs of the people who come to us. Like her, we at the Sanctuary believe that it is only when people see a solution that they realise there was a problem that needed a response. Like her, we at the Sanctuary welcome people of all faiths and none: all seekers and searchers are welcome, both on-site and online.

Sr Stan Kennedy and Sr Síle Wall

Reflection

Anniversaries are Made up of Memories

My first memory of the Sanctuary stretches back to 1999 and the clever design of the original meditation garden by Dominick Murphy, a fellow alumnus of the National Botanic Gardens College of Horticulture in Glasnevin. And again, it was a garden that brought the Sanctuary back into my life in 2020 when landscape artist Róisín Byrne commenced work designing the Biodiversity Field and Labyrinth, an urban oasis with impeccable environmental credentials. The Labyrinth was expertly constructed by O'Brien Landscaping, and it has become the Sanctuary's ode to the precarious state of our planet and a soothing balm for those who are anxious and overwhelmed by the climate emergency. There are many of us with these feelings.

As a true believer in the power of mindfulness, my time on the Sanctuary's board has reinforced my conviction that compassion for self is the foundation stone on which we build compassion and care for all sentient beings and all life on earth. I owe this renewed conviction to Jane Negrych's inspirational teachings and the impactful work of the Sanctuary that is so often facilitated and manifested by Sr Stan, Sr Síle, Tony Bates and other board members.

As the Sanctuary enters its next quarter-century, we need it more than ever. Congratulations to everyone who has worked so hard for twenty-five years and congratulations to all those who will carry the torch forward in the challenging times ahead.

Gary Graham, chairperson,
the Sanctuary board

Reflection   *The Best-Kept Secret*

I remember taking my first
mindfulness course in a yoga
studio in Phibsborough. This is
when I heard whisperings of a
haven in Stoneybatter called the
Sanctuary. It was almost as if I
had just been let in on the best-
kept secret. As part of the course,
we were to do our retreat day
there. The lady sitting next to me
told me that the Sanctuary was a
wonderful, serene space that went

beyond mindfulness. In her words, it had soul. Certainly, this has been my experience of being both a course participant and, more recently, the managing director of the Sanctuary. The Sanctuary has soul.

I have been working within the world of secular mindfulness for the past ten years. Before I came to work for the Sanctuary, I taught mindfulness and compassion and did teacher training throughout the United Kingdom and beyond. However, when I came to the Sanctuary, I could not ever have imagined the breadth or depth of work that I was about to embark on.

'Seeding our day with moments of stillness and peace'

Over my years in the Sanctuary, I have worked with Léargas and groups from the Central Remedial Clinic, exploring Kindness for Inclusion, and I have taught self-care to social workers, youth workers, teachers and Health Service Executive teams.

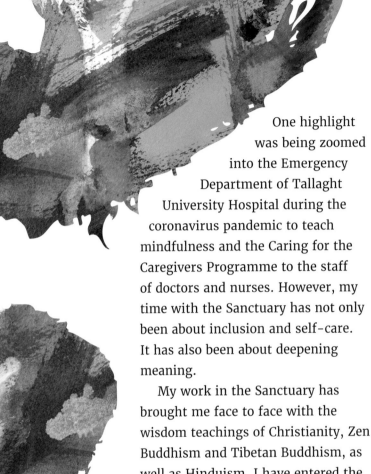

One highlight was being zoomed into the Emergency Department of Tallaght University Hospital during the coronavirus pandemic to teach mindfulness and the Caring for the Caregivers Programme to the staff of doctors and nurses. However, my time with the Sanctuary has not only been about inclusion and self-care. It has also been about deepening meaning.

My work in the Sanctuary has brought me face to face with the wisdom teachings of Christianity, Zen Buddhism and Tibetan Buddhism, as well as Hinduism. I have entered the desert, waited for the light and, most importantly, connected with my own inner sanctuary in a way that is not only profound but is also filled with a deep, unshakable peace.

I still teach secular mindfulness but have come to appreciate mindfulness from a Christian perspective and other faiths. I also teach compassion and perform teacher training within the walls of the Sanctuary. Only now do I really understand what the lady sitting next me meant that day. My teaching is enriched by the experiences of the people I meet, the wise teachings of spiritual traditions, and my own innate connection to all around and within me. The Sanctuary brings all these elements together. Moreover, the Sanctuary's soul beats within my work, moving me beyond mindfulness.

Jane Negrych, managing director,
the Sanctuary

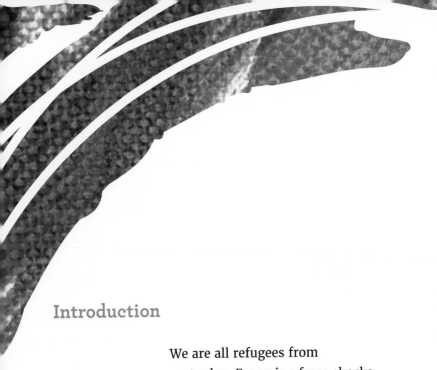

Introduction

We are all refugees from yesterday. Emerging from shocks, setbacks and losses, we gather ourselves and try to learn from what we've experienced. Sr Stan has felt those shocks more than most. She has witnessed the trauma of homelessness, the powerlessness of immigrants and the struggles of young people to find and be themselves in a world that is doing its best to make them somebody else. Her response to these injustices has been to create practical supports to meet the needs of our most vulnerable and uphold their dignity and human rights.

The Sanctuary is her and Sr Síle's response to a world that seems be lurching from one crisis to another. One may well ask what relevance a centre for mindfulness and compassion has to the anxiety and uncertainty we feel? To answer this, we need to recognise what living with chronic stress is doing to us all. Individually and collectively, we are in a constant state of emotional dysregulation. We are on edge, exhausted, and demoralised. Traditional institutions that helped maintain a sense of community and continuity have lost their relevance and their influence. We have become strangers to ourselves and to each other. We struggle with increasingly complex problems in a world where it's hard to find time

to connect with ourselves and the wisdom we need to survive.

The core activity of the Sanctuary, which is mindfulness meditation, is designed to enable people come home to themselves and connect with others and with Nature. When we are centred and connected, rather than anxious and unmoored, we can think clearly and creatively about what we can do to heal the world, or at least the particular corner of the world that is of concern to us.

The Sanctuary has helped me to become more grounded, more aware, and better able to manage my life. I feel more connected to the world around me and clearer about how I can make a difference.

Change begins with changing ourselves. Each of us can be the change we want to see in the world.

Tony Bates, Sanctuary board member

The Sanctuary Garden

Part 1

The Lodge, where the initial 'reflective meetings' were held

The Story of the Sanctuary

The Sanctuary is a centre of peace and meditation tucked away behind the Lodge at Stanhope Green, in the Stoneybatter/ Grangegorman area of Dublin. It is a place of beauty and stillness, where people can thrive and grow in awareness as they learn and practise meditation and mindfulness.

Based in the tradition of Christian meditation, and drawing on a wide range of spiritual practices, the Sanctuary welcomes people of all faiths and traditions, as well as people of no religious affiliation, to participate in its extensive programme of classes, courses, conferences, creative activities and retreats – in person at the Sanctuary itself, sometimes off-site and sometimes online.

'Setting aside time each day to be present, to be attentive, to be still'

How it started

As religious sisters themselves, Stanislaus Kennedy and Síle Wall, who were at the heart of the foundation of the Sanctuary, have always valued the practice of stopping, in the course of a busy day, to draw breath, to be quiet, to meditate or to pray. In her busy and often stressful work in the area of homelessness, Sr Stan always provided a quiet room, however small, in any building she worked in, where members of her team could withdraw from time to time to take a few moments' rest, to breathe, to be still, to meditate, or simply to sit and think – or to take a break from thinking.

Over time, this commitment to making quiet spaces in busy places led to the idea of creating such a place in the city, a place that could be shared with people in search of stillness, which would offer them the opportunity to learn and practise meditation in a calm, welcoming, supportive and beautiful environment. And so the idea of the Sanctuary began to form.

> 'I thought to myself, wouldn't it be great to create an oasis in the heart of Dublin, a place of rest and calm for the mind, body and spirit – a sanctuary. And that is what the Sanctuary is.'
>
> **Sr Stanislaus Kennedy,
> founder of the Sanctuary, 1998**

As sure as the idea for the Sanctuary grew out of a lifetime practice of providing quiet rooms in workplaces, that same idea flourished and evolved in collaboration with people who had all sorts of gifts to bring, and expertise and talents to share.

The initial 'reflective meetings' about what the Sanctuary might be were held in the Lodge, Stan and Síle's home, in the early months of 1997, and included some of their neighbours who were tenants of Focus Ireland's residential development, Stanhope Green, for people who have experienced homelessness. The Stanhope Green residents were asked to consider what ideas they might have about a quiet, local space that would be inclusive and welcoming.

'A supportive and gentle space where I can be myself and flourish.'

Sheila Gaffney, Sanctuary community member

Later that year, broader meetings were held, and a wider range of people with various kinds of expertise were invited to join. These meetings were reflective in nature, and sometimes took unusual forms; for example, a Sunday walk. The group also tried out some ideas themselves – Celtic spirituality and dreamwork were two of the areas that they explored together. These meetings came to an end when the Sanctuary was formally incorporated in the summer of 1998.

Creative evolution

There was no clearly developed plan for what the Sanctuary would do at first, but there was always the intention that it would offer support and spiritual sustenance, especially to people working on the front line with Focus Ireland, and later with others in the caring professions, in the conviction that nourishing and supporting people in their work would, in turn, have beneficial effects on the people they worked with. These days, what the Sanctuary has to offer is also available to the wider public.

'Walking through the doors of the Sanctuary there is a quietness, a stillness, a sense and a source of peace and comfort for those who come here.'

Johanne Farrelly, Sanctuary staff member

Everyone involved in those early meetings contributed their own gifts and talents, and so ideas and views emerged in conversation to inform the vision of Stan and Síle, who are still listening and learning a quarter-century later.

As Stan and Síle had intuited from the outset, the Sanctuary answered a hunger in people for spirituality, meditation, creativity and community – values that the Sanctuary has only recently identified and named as the four pillars of its purpose and vision.

> 'The Sanctuary for me is like stepping into a haven for my soul, an oasis held together by warm and inspiring people, a beautiful and serene environment along with heartfelt and enlightening course content. A true gift to the community.'
>
> **Ciara Holland, Sanctuary facilitator**

The building

As soon as it was decided that the Sanctuary would be built just behind the Lodge at Stanhope Green, on a plot of land leased from the Religious Sisters of Charity, plans started to be drawn up. Gerry Cahill, Jack Begley and Johnny Rooney worked with Stan and Síle to design the building, and Joe Powell of FÁS (the State training organisation at the time)

The Sacred Space

provided a team of people to do the construction work. The main classroom and workshop space, known as the Library, was the first area to be built. It is a conventional, practical room, big and versatile enough to host a variety of classes and activities.

Thought has always gone into making the Sanctuary a place that is physically as well as emotionally welcoming, and Stan and Síle wanted a meditation room and an inner sanctum, a Sacred Space, that would be especially calm, welcoming and soothing, and designed with 'no hard edges'. The meditation room, known as the Blue Room, and the inner Sacred Space, which adjoins it, are both circular in design, to give people using these spaces a sense of being held and safely enclosed.

*The Blue Room
meditation space*

'The "cloak" of the space wrapping around us all, giving opportunity for pause and reflection.'

Gerry Cahill, Sanctuary architect

The Blue Room is painted an intense blue, but the walls are otherwise unadorned and the furnishing is very simple, in keeping with its purpose as a room for quiet meditation. It is lit by three large and beautiful stained-glass windows, which were discovered in the Abbey Stained Glass Studios and restored by the Sanctuary. They were originally

located in Mount St Anne's in Dublin 6 and are almost two hundred years old. The windows are in the Christian stained-glass art tradition, and some people initially thought they made the place look 'too churchy', but over time people have come to appreciate their beauty and the sense of calm they bring to the room.

The small circular stained-glass window between the Sacred Space and the Blue Room

The Sacred Space itself has a small, circular, stained-glass window, in the wall between it and the Blue Room. Its main source of light is a lovely glass dome roof, through which sunshine pours in, and shadows play on the walls. It has tree-bark seating and wood sculptures. In addition to these main rooms, the Sanctuary also has some small consulting rooms, used for activities such as art therapy, along with a kitchen and offices.

> 'The building itself is very, very special, there's something in the walls of the Sanctuary that just breathe this air of peace and calm but mostly safety.'
>
> **Fiona O'Neill, Sanctuary facilitator**

The Sanctuary Garden

The building that houses the Sanctuary leads into a hidden walled garden, laid out in three circular areas, echoing the circular design of the Blue Room and the Sacred Space inside the building. The garden

The Sanctuary Garden

was designed and built by Dominick Murphy, and in 1999 the project was submitted for the government's Millennium Recognition Awards.

> 'The layout envisages three separate spaces: the Contemplative Garden, the Ornamental Garden and the Liturgy Garden, all leading from a central meeting area. It is designed to cater for all aspects of human interaction from quietness to conversation to group activities.'
>
> **From the submission to the Millennium Recognition Awards**

The Sanctuary Garden project was successful in this application and received a prize of over £36,000. In January 2001, the project was a finalist in the AIB Better Ireland Awards, in the heritage/environment category, and won £1,000.

The Contemplative Garden

*Garden tools ready
for gardening at the
Sanctuary*

In the early days, the Sanctuary relied on
donations of materials for construction and on
volunteers for labour. Stan and Síle approached John
Lonergan, the governor of Mountjoy Prison, asking
if he could supply a team of prisoners to lay out
the Sanctuary Garden. A small crew of men came
and, under supervision, built the garden paths and
fishpond – and a lovely job they made of it.

At one point, as the paths were being laid, Síle
had a brainwave. She collected some coloured glass
'stones' and scattered them into the cement between
the paving stones, before it set. They are there to this
day, glistening and winking in the garden's pathways.

'The Sanctuary is a very tranquil place with beautiful gardens – it truly is a Sanctuary.'

Sheila Caulfield, former Sanctuary board member

'For me the Sanctuary is a place of nature and beauty. An oasis of peace and calm in the heart of my old neighbourhood that assists my journey from head to heart. A compass point to guide me home.'

Colm Madigan, Sanctuary community member

'Moving from a place of stillness, we are more capable of having a right understanding, making right judgements and taking right actions'

Management and finances

The Sanctuary was incorporated as a company very early in its development, with a voluntary board of directors. Voluntary board members have come and gone over the years, all contributing valuable talent and expertise.

The work of the Sanctuary was originally based on a voluntary model. People like Gerry Cahill (architect), Jack Begley (engineer), Joe Lucey SDB (meditation teacher) and many, many others provided their services free of charge in areas such as web design, gardening, befriending, finances, building and design, and facilitation.

Activities were free of charge in the early days, and the informal drop-in meditation sessions, initially held on Wednesday evenings and later more frequently, have continued to be free of charge, whether in person or online, although participants may donate if they wish. Over time, it became necessary to charge people attending Sanctuary courses and activities, both in person and online, in order to cover costs. However, nobody has ever been turned away from the Sanctuary for financial reasons.

The Sanctuary has never had a secure source of finances. It has depended on divine providence and the goodwill of the people associated with it. Year

by year, the budget grew but the Sanctuary was able to make ends meet from its programmes, courses, events and voluntary donations.

Staff were part-time in the early years and were provided by FÁS, now known as the government's Community Employment scheme. The Sanctuary building was also built by FÁS under the direction of Joe Powell, a process that was designed to help people into the workforce.

In 2005, employment practices at the Sanctuary became more formalised. Niamh Bruce was appointed to manage the company and run its operations. When Niamh moved on after about ten years, a series of other managers took her place. Jane Negrych was appointed in 2019.

'Whether in the spring or winter of your life, a visit to the Sanctuary can offer a new beginning.'

John Robinson, Sanctuary staff member

Annual Conference on Mindfulness and Mental Health at Dublin Castle, 2010

Programmes and events

As early as 1999, the Sanctuary offered its first five-week course in meditation, 'The Art of Being Still', led by Joe Lucey, and in 2003 came the first day programmes, focusing on carers and their service users in Dublin's north inner city. By 2005, the Sanctuary was offering a range of courses and sessions, and a Sanctuary in Schools programme was already in development.

From 2010 to 2016, the Sanctuary ran a series of successful annual conferences on mindfulness, which were addressed by national and international speakers in Dublin Castle. The themes included the art of being still, mindfulness, well-being, mental health, and care and compassion.

An online conference to celebrate the Sanctuary's twenty-fifth anniversary was held in June 2023, when author and mindfulness teacher Sharon Salzberg joined Dr Tony Bates, British psychologist

Professor Paul Gilbert and Sr Stan to discuss how we might care for ourselves, for one another, and for the earth.

The Sanctuary went online during the COVID-19 pandemic. Like everywhere else, it had to close its doors and cease activities during the pandemic lockdowns. The Sanctuary responded quickly, however, and the Wednesday evening drop-in sessions, which had always been popular, went online. This meant that the sessions found a far bigger audience than could possibly ever have been physically accommodated in the Sanctuary itself. These online sessions took place three times per week and almost four thousand people registered for them in just two years. Having had to pivot quickly in response to the pandemic and offer online services, the Sanctuary now offered some of its programmes, courses and workshops as a hybrid model, with a mixture of in-person and online participants.

'I could never have imagined such a connection online and now it feels like an integral part of my life.'

Sanctuary community member

The Biodiversity Field and Labyrinth

In 2020, the Sanctuary leased a field, adjacent to the Sanctuary Garden, from the Religious Sisters of Charity, with a view to creating a labyrinth as a space for contemplative walking. Róisín Byrne was appointed as the designer. She worked on the project through the lockdowns, and would sometimes sit in the field and think about her vision for the space.

Unlike a formal maze made of high hedging and designed as a puzzle, the Sanctuary Labyrinth is designed as a sacred, meditative walk consisting of intricate paths, delineated by wildflower borders, through a grassy meadow. The design is inspired by the thirteenth-century labyrinth laid out in tiles on the floor of Chartres Cathedral in France.

The labyrinth in Chartres is contained within a single circle, but the

Aerial view of the Labyrinth designed by Róisín Byrne, Nature-Based Landscape Architecture. Image credit: Adam James

Sanctuary Labyrinth comprises three separate but connected circles, and a walker can walk one, two or all three of the circles. The first, medium-sized circle is entered from a blue limestone patio. From this circle, a path leads to a larger circle, but a walker can, if they wish, bypass this larger circle and move straight to the final and smallest circle. This final circle does not have a pathway in it, symbolising that you have arrived home. A walk can take anything from fifteen minutes to an hour, depending on the route taken and whether the walker stops to pray or meditate.

With biodiversity in mind, the meadow is planted with pollinator-friendly plants, organic where possible, in order to be in harmony with the earth's natural rhythms. As well as the Labyrinth, the meadow also has a small stand of fruit trees, along with some other native trees, mostly birch, and some holly. Climbing roses have been planted against one of the walls.

'Heaven in the middle of the city.'

Anita Dobulane,
Sanctuary staff member

Wooden benches, built by Paul Dempsey of Cork, are placed along the walks. The wood is Irish oak and it came from a single tree that blew down in Storm Darwin in 2014. The benches were gifted to the Sanctuary by a benefactor.

In 2022, Róisín's design won the Healthcare category at the Irish Landscape Institute Design Awards.

Ownership of the building and garden passed from the Religious Sisters of Charity to the Sanctuary in 2022, but the Biodiversity Meadow and Labyrinth continue to be leased on an annual basis.

Artwork in the Biodiversity Field by Ann Meldon Hugh

Part 2

Birds in the
Sanctuary Garden

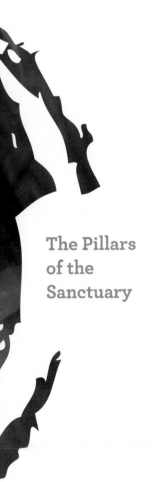

The Pillars of the Sanctuary

The Sanctuary's vision is to 'nourish personal growth for greater social impact'. In 2022, the development committee, a subcommittee of the Sanctuary board, identified four pillars of the Sanctuary:

» Spirituality
» Meditation
» Creativity, and
» Community.

The board also agreed, in December 2022, that the aspirations of the Sanctuary are to:

» EMBODY compassion, stillness, beauty, creativity and spirituality
» ENABLE people to develop self-awareness, which is fundamental to growth and healing, and
» CONNECT people more compassionately with themselves and their environment, community and society.

Although the four pillars have only recently been named, they have always been at the core of what the Sanctuary does. They are dealt with separately here, but in reality, of course, they work seamlessly together.

'The Sanctuary for me is a grace-filled place of beauty, hope and stillness. It has been lovingly tended by so many carers over the years. I see it as a refuge and invitation to live a more peaceful, connected and meaningful life, a real gift in a troubled world.'

John Doherty, facilitator

*Walking the Labyrinth
in the Biodiversity Field*

» Spirituality

The Sanctuary's core work is to offer courses in mindfulness and meditation: it is essentially a place of spiritual practice. With the Sacred Space at its still centre, and the sacred walk of the Labyrinth at its edge, every activity in the Sanctuary draws on a deep well of spirituality.

The Sanctuary's activities have generally emerged from Christian spirituality, but it has always been open to, and welcomes people from, a wide range of spiritual traditions.

*Stained glass casting light
in the Sacred Space*

'The Sanctuary is for people of all religions,
cultures or ethos. This creates the richness of
the Sanctuary.'

Niamh Bruce, manager of the Sanctuary, 2005

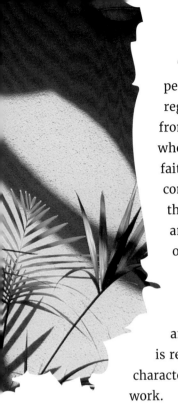

The Sanctuary wants to help people find meaning in their lives, regardless of the spiritual tradition from which they come and whether or not they are people of faith. The Sanctuary's passionate commitment to bringing together the spiritual traditions of East and West, and Christianity and other world faiths, is at the heart of its appeal to a wide range of students, supporters and practitioners of meditation and mindfulness. This openness is recognised as a defining characteristic of the Sanctuary and its work.

Christian tradition

The Sanctuary has always been rooted in the Christian faith and tradition. From very early on, Br Richard Hendrick has been spiritual advisor to the Sanctuary and continues to be hugely influential. He is a major influence in the development of the youth programme and in the history and teachings of Christian meditation and mindfulness.

Ashram

Sr Stan visited an ashram run by Fr Korko Moses SJ in the south of India in 2009. She then invited Korko Moses to come to Ireland and conduct a summer ashram. In 2011, a group of volunteers was convened to plan a residential, ashram-style retreat to be run by the Sanctuary with Korko Moses over a period of four weeks, with people attending for a few days' retreat.

The Sanctuary itself could not accommodate such a programme, so an arrangement was made to hold the ashram at the Stella Maris Retreat Centre in Howth (north of Dublin). The first ashram was held in 2012, and was so successful that it ran annually until the pandemic.

'Every new day is an opportunity to delight in life'

6.45 a.m.	Yoga–asana (conference room)
7.30 a.m.	Prayers/chants and meditation (meditation room)
8.30 a.m.	Breakfast
9 a.m.	Karma yoga 1: Services in awareness
10.30 a.m.	Meditation input session 1, followed by meditation
12.30 p.m.	Lunch/rest
	Personal sadhana (personal spiritual practices)
2.30 p.m.	Meditation input session 2, followed by meditation
3.45 p.m.	Karma yoga 2: Services in awareness
4.45 p.m.	Break
5.15 p.m.	Bhajan singing, meditation, Arati
6 p.m.	Supper
7 p.m.	Satsangh: Sharing the day's experiences/ time for questions and answers
8 p.m.	Close – personal sādhanā (personal spiritual practices)

*Dawn Chorus event in the
Sanctuary Garden, 2022.
Image credit: Kevin Hegarty*

Celebrating the seasons

Since the very beginning, the Sanctuary has had a
tradition of singing carols at Christmas. This had to
stop when the COVID-19 pandemic hit in 2020 and,
instead, a series of talks called 'Waiting for the Light'
was made available online on the four Saturdays
before Christmas. Although the focus is on the
Christian festival, speakers of other faiths also take
part.

The Sanctuary has also held a series of 'Preparing
for Easter' talks for many years, and, in 2020, hosted
its first Dawn Chorus event, celebrating birdsong in a
special, mindful way. In 2023, the first year in which

'Breathing in and breathing out thanksgiving, peace, joy'

St Brigid's Day was honoured by the Irish State as a public holiday, the Sanctuary marked the occasion by hosting the start of Brigid's Way Imbolc Pilgrimage, as part of the Clondalkin Lá Fhéile Bríde Imbolc Festival.

Plum Village

The Sanctuary has long had an association with the revered Zen master Thich Nhat Hanh (now deceased) and his International Plum Village Community of Engaged Buddhism in Bordeaux, France. Monks from there have been visiting the Sanctuary since

Plum Village monks at a meditation event in St Laurence's Church, Grangegorman, TU Dublin

the early days and they continued to come until COVID-19. It started with Sr Gina, an Irish Buddhist and assistant to Thich Nath Nanh in Plum Village, who visited two years in succession with some members of her community, after which other monks and nuns from her community also started to visit the Sanctuary every year. They often participated by leading the Wednesday evening drop-in sessions, and people flocked to the Sanctuary when they were there. They have generously continued their support of the Sanctuary's work online and have taken part in the 'Waiting for the Light' and 'Preparing for Easter' talks.

'The more peace in us, the more peace in the world'

*Fr Joe Lucey's
singing bowl*

» Meditation

Meditation is the core activity
practised in the Sanctuary
and classes in meditation and
mindfulness have always been its
main offering.

The Art of Being Still

Fr Joe Lucey taught his first five-
week meditation course, 'The Art
of Being Still', in 1999, and he
continued to teach that course
twice yearly for several years.
By 2005, the Sanctuary was also
offering five mindfulness days

throughout the year, as well as a weekly support group for meditators. This evolved into what are known as the 'Wednesday evening drop-in sessions'.

> 'I often go back in my mind to learning to sit in meditation in the Blue Room with the late Joe Lucey – a shining light from those early days that has not dimmed after all these years.'
>
> **Mary Jennings, Sanctuary facilitator**

When Joe Lucey sadly died, far too young, in 2007, Sr Stan felt she might be able to take on the programme he had developed. And so, with the psychologist Tony Bates, a long-time friend of the Sanctuary, she visited a Buddhist meditation centre in rural Scotland. They learned about how to structure meditation sessions, and what they learned in Scotland particularly informed how the drop-in sessions – which had grown out of Joe's courses – were organised. Over time, some of the regular participants in these sessions were invited to lead them. Stan also started teaching Joe's 'Art of Being Still' course herself after the visit to Scotland.

Other courses developed from there and today the Sanctuary offers a wide range of courses in meditation and mindfulness, while the 'Wednesday evening drop-in sessions' now take place online – and not only on Wednesdays.

'The beauty we nourish within ourselves creates a beautiful world'

'I used to think years ago that meditation was a brilliant "idea", a great way to relax, but since practising I have realised that it is a way of life, a way of choosing to live.'

**Michael Connolly,
Sanctuary Garden volunteer**

Sanctuary for Young People

In addition to its core offering of courses and 'drop-in' meditation sessions for adults, the Sanctuary has provided mindfulness programmes to schoolchildren for many years. The Sanctuary for Young People (S4YP) programme evolved over several years and teachers, youth workers, creative artists, parents and wisdom teachers have participated.

> 'In a world where the young people I teach have more anxiety, pressure and expectation, the Awareness Days at The Sanctuary act as a reminder. A reminder of who they truly are, in that moment – whole, unbroken and perfect. I can visibly see them unclench and unfurl in the calm that embraces them in Dublin's best-kept secret!'
>
> **Frances O'Brien, teacher**

S4YP was designed as three distinct but integrated modules – exploration, creativity and communication. It was offered at three levels: 'the Wisdom Journey', 'the Warrior Journey' and 'the Wonderment Journey'. It also initiated Awareness Days, which included the creation of mandalas in the classroom or youth club or at the Sanctuary itself.

'What happens when I go in to the Sanctuary … I start to feel joy.'

Mindful Warrior Programme participant, 2022

A core element of S4YP is the Mindful Warrior Programme, devised by Br Richard Hendrick, with the assistance of Niamh Bruce, manager of the Sanctuary at the time. This programme continued to run until the COVID-19 pandemic began and is now being revised; the Awareness Days recommenced in 2022.

'The Sanctuary retreat was an amazing experience and one I would recommend to everyone. Accessible, interactive and genuinely interesting, my year and I didn't just learn skills to cope with school, we learned skills to cope with life.'

Siofra Delaney, student attending Awareness Day

I Can Feel My Toes Breathe: Bringing Meditation and Stillness to Young People, a handbook that was compiled by Br Richard and the Sanctuary, based on the Mindful Warrior Programme, was published by Veritas in 2010. From 2012 to 2022, the Sanctuary was also involved with a UK programme known as the Mindfulness in Schools Project, which involved running training courses that enabled school staff and others working in youth-related fields to teach the .b classroom-based mindfulness programme for 11–18-year-olds and the Paws.b curriculum for 7–11-year-olds.

The Sanctuary developed a partnership with the National Youth Council of Ireland in 2010, and designed a programme for youth leaders to introduce meditation and mindfulness to the young people they worked with, as well as into their own lives. This partnership continues today.

'The presence I bring to any moment gives it power to bless, to nourish; to change an ordinary unnoticed moment into a moment of beauty feeding the soul'

These initiatives led to the Sanctuary's Caring for the Caregivers Programme offering support to those in the caring professions, from working on the front lines in our health services to child and family support workers and many more.

'Being in the Sanctuary and spending time together and knowing the inspirational story of collective contributions and support of a shared belief in something, this is a nourishing connection to the work we do here together – it calms and nourishes my spirit and connects me to the bigger community and movement of those working for social justice.'

LGBT Ireland Peer Support Group member

Sanctuary for young people – making a mandala

» Creativity

Although the main work of the Sanctuary concentrates on mindfulness and meditation practice, there has always been a commitment to creativity: creativity in how the Sanctuary itself was conceived and developed; creativity in the design and decoration of the physical space, both indoors and outdoors; creativity in how Sanctuary activities have evolved over time, especially recently in response to the restrictions imposed during the pandemic; and creativity in the sense of offerings based on the arts. Indeed, everything that goes on in the Sanctuary is constantly in a dynamic, creative state of evolution.

Art therapy

Síle Wall has a background in art therapy, and worked with a small, local arts centre for a couple of years before the establishment of the Sanctuary. She is particularly committed to fostering creativity in what the Sanctuary does, and for many years offered art therapy there. She has now retired but one-on-one art therapy sessions for children and adults are still held at the Sanctuary.

Spiritual odysseys

Over many years, the Sanctuary ran workshops that were referred to as 'spiritual odysseys'. These took place on Saturday mornings and were very well attended. Artists from a range of disciplines led workshops, in pottery (Donagh O'Shea), song and music (Christy Moore, Noirín Ní Riain and John Buckley, among others), and poetry (the late Brendan Kennelly, Paula Meehan and many others), and all offered their services free of charge. These workshops helped to extend the reach of the

Artists who attended the Spiritual Odyssey event in 2006: Brendan Kennelly (left); Luka Bloom (centre); Christy Moore (right)

Sanctuary. There is no plan to resume these 'spiritual odysseys' at the moment; however, we hope that these or similar events will be part of the life of the Sanctuary going forward.

The Sanctuary has also hosted sessions on creative writing, creative expression, creative dance, chanting and Tai-Chi Quan. Since 2022, the Biodiversity Meadow is used for yoga, weather permitting. There is currently a wealth of creative courses on offer at the Sanctuary such as 'Finding Peace in Nature', 'Mindfulness and Music' and 'Yoga and Trauma', to name but a few.

*Yoga in the Biodiversity Meadow
during the Stoneybatter Festival, 2022*

'The Sanctuary is the well I return to again and again to replenish my soul.'

Tony Hickey, yoga participant

Book club
The Sanctuary held a book club, the Léacht club, in 2013–14, which met every two months on Sunday mornings. Members agreed on the book to be read in advance of the meeting, and then, at the Sunday

'Our spiritual life is a life of love, of listening and responding, of giving and receiving'

morning session at the Sanctuary, shared what resonated with them about the book in relation to their own practice – what they found new, insightful or interesting.

Christmas concerts

In 1999, a Christmas carol celebration with the Dublin Gospel Choir was held for staff and friends of the Sanctuary. This developed into an annual evening of music, song and poetry, compered generously every year by RTÉ's Marty Whelan. As numbers grew, the Christmas concert was moved to the premises of the Law Society in nearby Blackhall Place and became a fundraising event for the Sanctuary as well as a social occasion for the Sanctuary community.

Frances Black, Mary Black, Luka Bloom, Mary Coughlan, Colm Mac Con Iomaire, Paula Meehan, Nóirín Ní Riain, Aoife Scott and John Sheehan are just some of the artists who have performed at this event.

The pandemic forced the Christmas concert to stop but plans are now in place to resume it for 2023.

Works of art

Many wonderful pieces of art have been gifted to the Sanctuary over the years. Each gift assists the Sanctuary in creating moments of surprise, beauty, inspiration and opportunity for visitors as they stop, pause, reflect and become still.

> 'The Sanctuary to me is peace. It's a space to breathe, to learn, to share, to stop and stare, to listen to sounds. It's a place to be, to return home to myself, to return to each wonderful moment.'
>
> **Robert Quinn, Sanctuary community member**

» Community

The Sanctuary was originally established with the idea of providing spiritual sustenance to those associated with Focus Ireland, and its very first community was comprised of local residents in Stanhope Green and people working on the front line with Focus Ireland. Nowadays, the Sanctuary has a much broader remit and links with many communities.

'Hope grows as life emerges from the darkness of the earth'

'The Sanctuary is a rich and diverse community of mindfulness practitioners, a constantly evolving ecosystem of educators, mental health experts, health workers, caregivers and social and environmental activists, where we grow and flourish together, learning how to practise engaged mindfulness and compassion.'

Mike Kavanagh, Sanctuary community member

Staff, volunteer and facilitator gathering, 2022

The breadth of the Sanctuary's vision and its openness to all spiritual traditions, along with its varied creative activities such as contemporary dance in the garden, chanting, song and poetry, attract individuals and groups, of all ages. There are still people coming to the Sanctuary who have been associated with it since the very beginning, a quarter of a century ago.

'The Sanctuary was a saving grace for me and got me out on the road to recovery after my experience of cancer in 1999.'

Pat McManamly, Sanctuary community member

Outreach

Reaching out to the neighbourhood was always a core part of the Sanctuary's mission. Knowing the history of the Religious Sisters of Charity's involvement with the Grangegorman hospital and workhouse since the early nineteenth century, Stan and Síle approached the senior psychiatric consultant in the former St Brendan's Hospital, Grangegorman, to discuss the needs of people living with mental health issues in the area.

> 'The journey with the Sanctuary has enhanced my life, professionally and personally, emotionally and spiritually – it's a holistic thing. I have received so much over the years and am delighted to give something back through Befriending. I feel so privileged and grateful. *Míle buíochas.*'
>
> **Mary Healy, Befriending volunteer**

Following on from this, in 2010 the Sanctuary decided to form a team of 'Befrienders' who would visit local mental health community residences on a weekly basis, offering friendship and support and accompanying many of them on social outings. This Befriending Service continues to work really well

with support from the Health Service Executive (HSE) social-work team. The Befriending volunteers would say that they receive more than they give.

'The Sanctuary's Befriending project has been a lifeline to our residents who are some of the most vulnerable and socially isolated in the community. The volunteers provide social connection and companionship and it has been wonderful to see these relationships develop.'

Aoife Farrelly, HSE mental-health social worker

Helping maintain the garden is normally also part of the Sanctuary's outreach programme, with volunteers coming one day per month since the beginning, except for during the COVID-19 lockdown years.

Group in the Sanctuary, 2023

Much of the community activity that occurs in and around the Sanctuary is spontaneous and informal. For example, in the past, children from the special class in a local Educate Together school would come regularly to walk around, meet the dogs and see the fish. The presence of the dogs has added to the life and spirit of the Sanctuary and they are a source of comfort and solace to many. This kind of casual but meaningful connection with the community in which it finds itself is typical of the Sanctuary's ethos.

As people started to discover the Sanctuary in the early days, they began to form their own communities; in particular, the people who attended

'Rebuilding our relationship with the earth, we hear the earth's song, we know its harmony and realise its connection with us'

the Wednesday evening drop-in sessions often formed social groups outside the Sanctuary. Similarly, people who attend the annual conferences often go on to form social connections and friendships after meeting like-minded people at these events.

Seasonal events

Christmas concerts (which evolved from simple carol singing in the early days into full evenings of poetry and music) are held in the annual run-up to Christmas. These annual celebrations have been an important focus over the years for everyone associated with the Sanctuary, and they make a major contribution to the Sanctuary's sense of community, as well as providing an important means of fundraising.

The Sanctuary opens its doors to the public each year during the local Stoneybatter Festival, and it was open also in 2018, on the occasion of the Religious Sisters of Charity celebrating two hundred years of their congregation in Stoneybatter.

Sanctuary in schools

While piloting the Mindful Warrior Programme in 2005, the Sanctuary formed links with three local schools: St Paul's CBS, North Brunswick Street; St Joseph's Secondary School, Stanhope Street; and Larkin Community College, Cathal Brugha Street.

In 2012, a steering group was established to explore new ways the Sanctuary might interact with schools and schoolchildren, and working with children is now an important activity of the Sanctuary.

Sanctuary at TU Dublin

In 2014, the Sanctuary community was once again expanded when it was invited by the chaplain at the Dublin Institute of Technology (DIT: now Technological University Dublin, or TU Dublin) to lead mindfulness sessions at lunchtime, once a week, for staff, students and local people, in St Laurence's Church on the Grangegorman campus. Weekly mindfulness sessions were later led by the Sanctuary in TU Dublin venues on Aungier Street and Bolton Street.

Mindfulness in Schools training course participants, 2022

During the pandemic, these sessions continued online, resuming in person in Grangegorman and Bolton Street in 2022 and, since 2023, in Aungier Street and Tallaght. These informal sessions were initially provided on a voluntary basis; these days, the facilitators are paid.

Sometime later, the Sanctuary was asked by DIT, as it was then, to develop a level 7 module, 'An Introduction to Mindfulness', which was delivered in DIT's School of Languages, Law and Social Sciences in 2017–18. This was an introductory module aimed at students who wished to grow their understanding and practice of mindfulness by developing 'the capacity to use mindfulness practice to deepen skills of reflection in academic life and in personal and professional relationships' (a projected learning outcome from this module).

Being Present course training, 2022

Sanctuary and IMA

The Sanctuary has had a fruitful partnership with
IMA (Institute for Mindfulness-Based Approaches),
an international organisation for training teachers
in mindfulness founded by Linda Lehrhaupt in 2001.
This was the first mindfulness training for teachers
offered in Ireland. Many Sanctuary staff have trained
with IMA at no cost.

This partnership led the Sanctuary to host the
MBCL (Mindfulness–Based Compassionate Living)
programme established by Erik van den Brink
and Frits Koster. A number of staff members and
other individuals completed this programme at the

Sanctuary over a period of eighteen months to become teachers of compassion.

This partnership was replaced in 2018 when the Sanctuary entered a franchisee agreement with the Mindfulness Association in the UK. Since then, Jane Negrych (Sanctuary managing director) has been delivering the Mindfulness-Based Living Course (MBLC) teacher training, as well as its in-depth mindfulness training, at the Sanctuary.

'Take the time to stop, look, observe. Beauty surrounds us'

In 2022, the MBLC was acknowledged by the MTAI (Mindfulness Teachers Association of Ireland) as meeting its Good Practice Guidelines, and the Sanctuary's teacher training course is now listed on the MTAI website.

The Sanctuary and the University of Aberdeen

The Sanctuary is currently working in partnership with the University of Aberdeen in Scotland on a National Institute for Health and Care Research project to train teacher educators in Rwanda and Ethiopia. These teacher educators will then introduce mindfulness to student teachers and rural schools in these countries. The project is planned to run for four years, from 2022 to 2026, and will be delivered online (one week in 2023 will take place in Rwanda).

Australian visitors to the Sanctuary, 2018

Poem

*The Sanctuary's Flowering
Quince Remembers*

Síle Wall

Twenty-three years ago
the Sanctuary
became my home.
A quiet space.
A silent space.
A still space.

Rooting, settling,
waiting, pausing,
listening.

Earth's natural rhythms
nourishing.
A rich tapestry
interweaving
threads
of colour and surprise
around me.

Wednesday evening
footfalls
one step following another
I have arrived
I am home
pathways echoing
stained glass shimmering
feet touching earth.

Blackbird nesting.
My tangly thorny branches
creating safety
hidden deep.

Beauty alive
buds, blooms, fallen leaves, resting soil
laughter and sorrow
music, poetry, song

water sound
bird sound
breath sound.
Life's miracle
visible
to my
invisible presence
supported by a north-east-facing wall.

The aliveness of memory.
My surroundings
constantly
a dynamic
creative state
of evolution.

The wonder of life
the gift of life
year by year
day by day
moment by moment.
I'm breathing
part of the big breath of life.

A wooden bench, made from Irish oak, in the Sanctuary Garden

Conclusion

Writing this short history of the Sanctuary has been a wonderful, mind-opening journey of reminiscence that we are proud to have been part of. It has been an experience that illustrates the generosity of people in the past and the great potential and possibility for the future.

Indeed, as we look to the future, we hope to continue to offer this quiet place for those who are looking for a space to find stillness, to resource themselves with the beauty of nature, the practice of meditation, and the grace of compassion. For it is through taking care of ourselves that we are able to care for one another, including this beautiful planet. We plan on renewing our dedication to working towards creating a more compassionate, just and resilient world.

May all beings be happy
May all beings live with an open heart
May all beings feel the tenderness of belonging.

Metta Bhavana Prayer